FINGERSTYLE Ukulele

by Fred Sokolow

To access audio visit:
www.halleonard.com/mylibrary

Enter Code
7079-4263-3564-5912

with editorial assistance by Ronny Schiff

ISBN 978-1-4584-2311-5

HAL•LEONARD® CORPORATION

7777 W. BLUEMOUND RD. P.O. BOX 13819 MILWAUKEE, WI 53213

In Australia Contact:
Hal Leonard Australia Pty. Ltd.
4 Lentara Court
Cheltenham, Victoria, 3192 Australia
Email: ausadmin@halleonard.com.au

Visit Hal Leonard Online at
www.halleonard.com

Contents

Introduction

If you're one of the nine million YouTube viewers who watched Jake Shimabukuro's amazing performance of "While My Guitar Gently Weeps," if you've seen James Hill turn his ukulele into an R&B band playing "Billy Jean," or heard Ohta-San play "Claire de Lune," you know that the ukulele can be much more than a strumming, sing-along instrument. As far back as the 1920s, popular American artists like Roy Smeck and Cliff Edwards (Ukulele Ike), and Hawaiians like Ernest Ka'ai raised the bar and showed the world that the ukulele could be a solo instrument like a piano or a guitar. The ukulele can shine on instrumental versions of popular songs, rock, jazz, classical music, and anything else you can imagine.

If you want to take your ukulele playing to the next level and learn how to play beautiful instrumentals, you need to start using your fingers! The sample songs and patterns found in this book and recording will get you started both playing solos and accompaniment—fingerstyle.

You will learn how to use your right-hand fingers and thumb to play chord melody solos on the ukulele; mixing chords and single notes like a pianist or a guitarist. You will also learn fingerpicking accompaniment patterns for a variety of textures and rhythmic grooves. Because fingerstyle playing works for all genres, folk, jazz, blues, and country songs are included in this collection.

Happy strumming... and picking!

ABOUT THE AUDIO

All ukulele parts are panned to one side of the stereo mix, so you can isolate them for close study, or pan them out and play along with the band.

All instruments: Fred Sokolow

Recorded at Sossity Sound by Michael Monagan

Fingerstyle Accompaniment

If you've only *strummed* the ukulele, the accompaniment patterns in this chapter will introduce you to *fingerpicking*. You'll learn a number of ways to accompany different types of songs with various rhythmic grooves.

The fingers of your picking hand will be labeled throughout the book using the standard Spanish letters, p-i-m-a:

p (pulgar) = thumb
i (indicio) = index finger
m (medio) = middle finger
a (anular) = ring finger

THUMB AND TWO-FINGER UP-PICK: CUT TIME

Here's a very simple picking pattern for *cut time*, a rhythmic feel that's especially useful in country, folk, or bluegrass music. It may also work for blues, Tin Pan Alley, or rock tunes as well.

- Pick the fourth string with your thumb (p).
- Pick the second and first strings simultaneously with your index (i) and middle (m) fingers.
- Pick the third string with your thumb.
- Pick the second and first strings simultaneously with your index and middle fingers.

TRACK 1

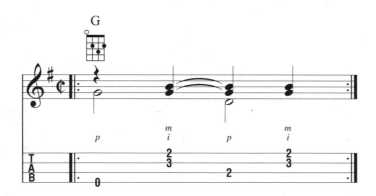

Use the pattern to play the following old country/folk train song, "Wabash Cannonball," which was popularized by the Carter Family, and later by Roy Acuff.

TRACK 2

WABASH CANNONBALL — ACCOMPANIMENT

Lis - ten   to   the jin - gle,   to the rum - ble and the
might - y rush of the en - gines,   in the lone - some ho - bo's

roar,   as she glides a - long the wood - lands   through the
call,   trav - el - in' through   the jun - gles on   the

hills and   by the shore.   Hear the ball.
Wa - bash   Can - non -

The same picking pattern can be used in old, cut time jazz standards like "Avalon," which was a huge hit for Al Jolson in 1921. The thumb is reversed in the following arrangement.

- Pick the third string with your thumb.
- Pick the second and first strings simultaneously with your index and middle fingers.
- Pick the fourth string with your thumb.
- Pick the second and first strings simultaneously with your index and middle fingers.

 TRACK 3 (0:00)

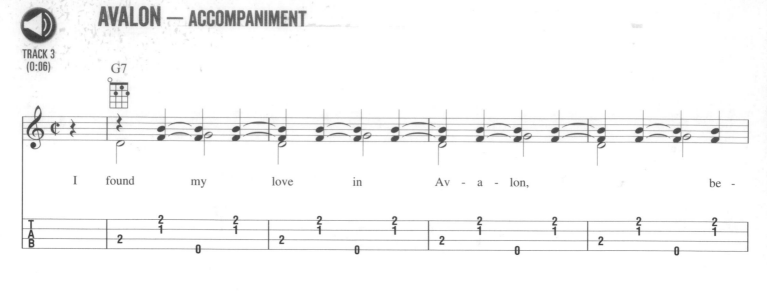

I found my love in Av - a - lon, be -

side the bay. I

left my love in Av - a - lon, and

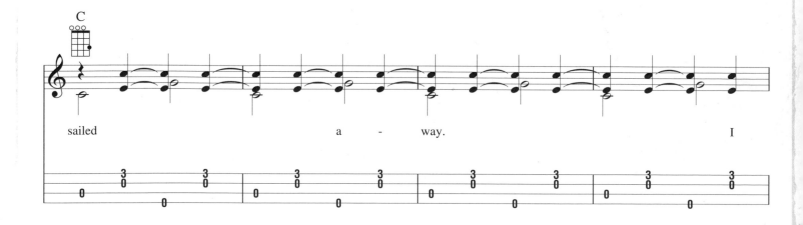

sailed a - way. I

THUMB AND TWO-FINGER UP-PICK: WALTZ TIME

You can adapt this accompaniment pattern to waltz (3/4) time.

- Pick the fourth string with your thumb.
- Pick the second and first strings simultaneously with your index and middle fingers.
- Pick the second and first strings again.
- Pick the third string with your thumb.
- Pick the second and first strings simultaneously with your index and middle fingers.
- Pick the second and first strings again.

TRACK 4

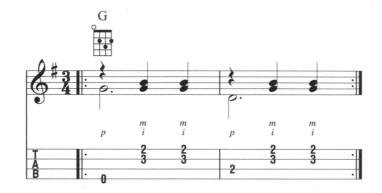

The following version of "Take Me Out to the Ball Game" makes use of this waltz pattern.

TRACK 5

TAKE ME OUT TO THE BALL GAME — ACCOMPANIMENT

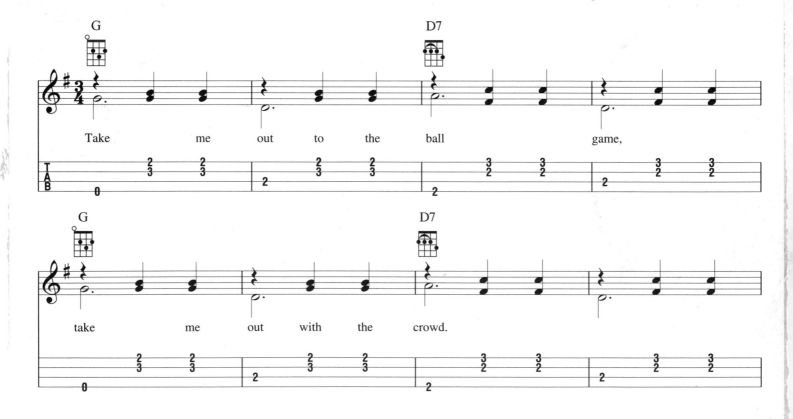

A PATTERN FOR SLOWER WALTZ TIME

Here's a fancier waltz pattern that makes use of the thumb and three fingers. It works nicely on slower 3/4 time songs. Play it a few times, then try it on the old gospel tune, "Amazing Grace."

- Pick the fourth string with your thumb.
- Pick the third string with your index finger.
- Pick the second and first strings simultaneously, with the middle and ring (a) fingers.
- Pick the third string with your index finger.
- Pick the second and first strings simultaneously with your middle and ring fingers.
- Pick the third string with your index finger.

TRACK 6
(0:00)

TRACK 6
(0:07)

AMAZING GRACE — ACCOMPANIMENT

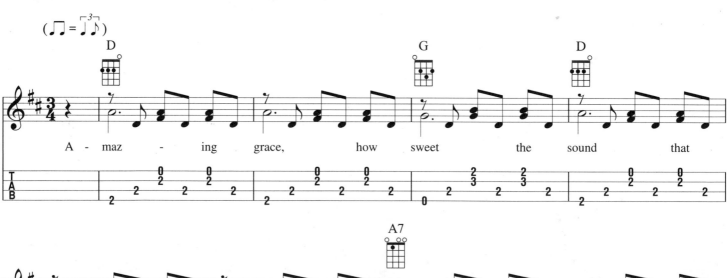

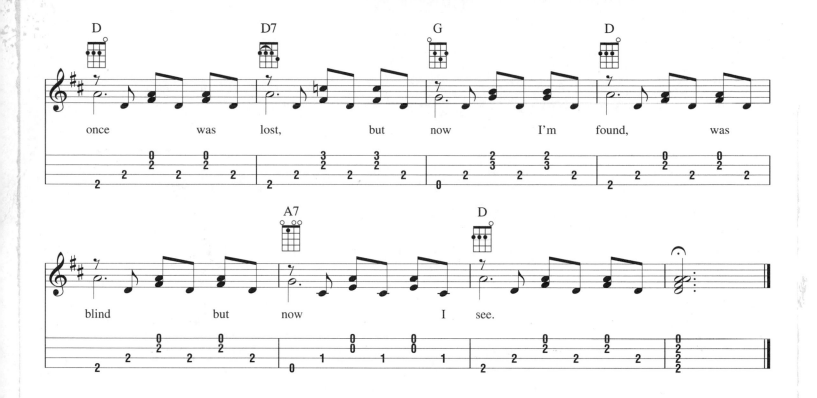

once   was   lost,   but   now   I'm   found,   was

blind   but   now   I   see.

THUMB AND TWO-FINGER UP-PICK: A SHUFFLE BEAT

"Amazing Grace" (Track 6) has a *shuffle beat* or "dotted-note" rhythmic feel. The eighth notes are performed in a "skipping" rhythm, in which the first of every two eighth notes is emphasized and held longer than the second (ONE and TWO and THREE and). You can shorten the waltz pattern to play a 4/4 time shuffle beat like the one found on the old blues/jazz tune, "After You've Gone."

- Pick the fourth string with your thumb.
- Pick the third string with your index finger.
- Pick the second and first strings simultaneously, with the middle and ring fingers.
- Pick the third string with your index finger.

TRACK 7
(0:00)

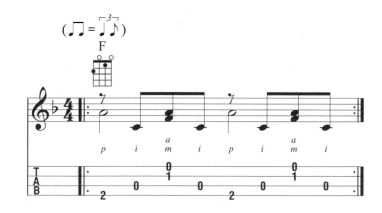

AFTER YOU'VE GONE — ACCOMPANIMENT

THUMB AND TWO-FINGER UP-PICK: STRAIGHT EIGHTHS TIME

The same pattern can be played in *straight eighths* time in country or rock tunes. Try it in the following version of "Stagolee," a blues tune that has been recorded by many rock and R&B bands.

STAGOLEE — ACCOMPANIMENT

TRACK 8

THREE-FINGER ROLLS: A SHUFFLE BEAT

Though they're called *three-finger rolls*, the following fingerpicking patterns are really played with the thumb and two fingers (the index and middle).

Here's a three-finger shuffle beat with the same feel as Track 7. After playing the pattern several times, play the old blues standard, "Careless Love."

- Pick the third string with your thumb.
- Pick the second string with your index finger.
- Pick the fourth string with your thumb.
- Pick the first string with your middle finger.

TRACK 9
(0:00)

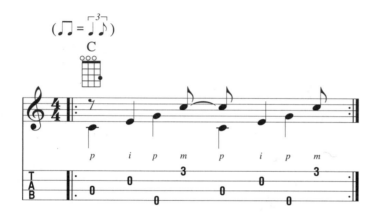

TRACK 9
(0:08)

CARELESS LOVE — ACCOMPANIMENT

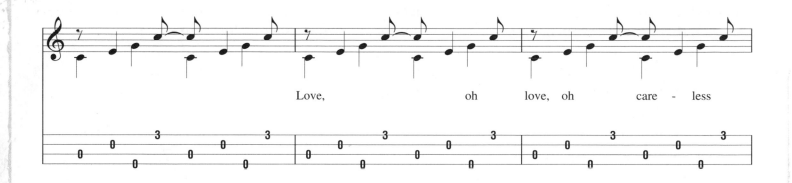

Love,   oh   love, oh   care - less

love,   love,   oh

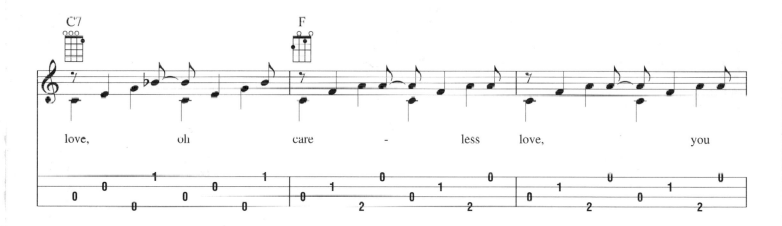

love,   oh   care   -   less   love,   you

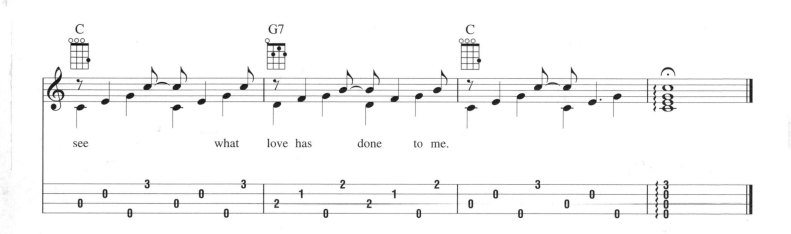

see   what   love has   done   to   me.

THREE-FINGER ROLLS: STRAIGHT EIGHTHS TIME

The previous pattern can also be played with a straight eighths feel in tunes like the old ballad, "Shenandoah." However, this version of "Shenandoah" makes use of the following—slightly different—pattern.

- Pick the third string with your thumb.
- Pick the second string with your index finger.
- Pick the first string with your middle finger.
- Pick the second string with your index finger.
- Pick the fourth string with your thumb.
- Pick the second string with your index finger.
- Pick the first string with your middle finger.
- Pick the second string with your index finger.

TRACK 10
(0:00)

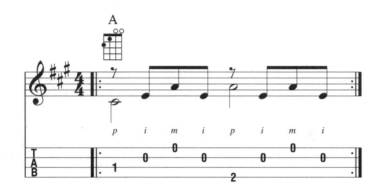

SHENANDOAH — ACCOMPANIMENT

TRACK 10
(0:09)

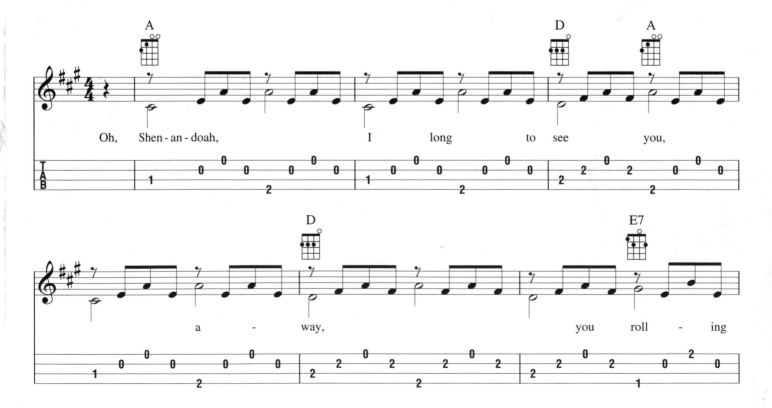

THREE-FINGER ROLLS: A CALYPSO FEEL

This three-finger roll—borrowed from bluegrass banjo—has a Calypso feel. Try it on the old folk tune, "Sloop John B.," popularized by the Beach Boys. Then, try it on classic rock tunes like "Proud Mary" or R&B classics like "Stand by Me" and "Under the Boardwalk."

- Pick the second string with your index finger.
- Pick the first string with your middle finger.
- Pick the fourth string with your thumb.
- Pick the second string with your index finger.
- Pick the first string with your middle finger.
- Pick the fourth string with your thumb.
- Pick the third string with your index finger.
- Pick the first string with your middle finger.

TRACK 11
(0:00)

TRACK 11
(0:08)

SLOOP JOHN B. — ACCOMPANIMENT

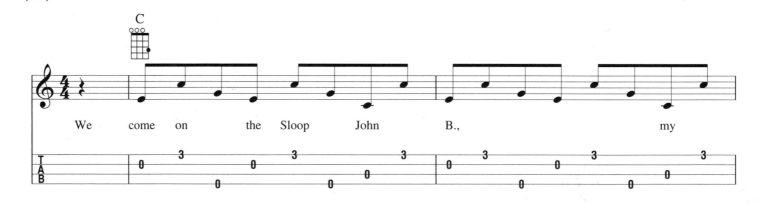

We come on the Sloop John B., my

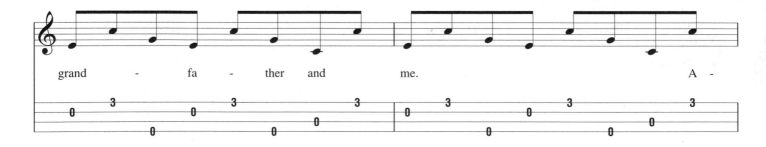

grand - fa - ther and me. A -

THREE-FINGER ROLLS: WALTZ TIME

There are many ways to fingerpick 3/4 time accompaniment. Here are two different patterns that are both used in the old cowboy tune, "I Ride an Old Paint." It starts with the first pattern and ends with the second pattern. Use a shuffle feel for that authentic cowboy saunter.

First Pattern:
- Pick the second string with your index finger.
- Pick the first string with your middle finger.
- Pick the fourth string with your thumb.
- Pick the second string with your index finger.
- Pick the first string with your middle finger.
- Pick the fourth string with your thumb.

Second Pattern:
- Repeat all six strokes replacing the second string/index finger with the third string/index finger.

TRACK 12
(0:00)

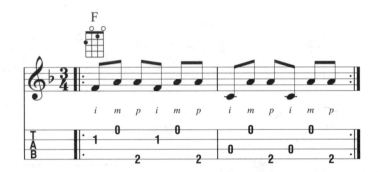

TRACK 12
(0:10)

I RIDE AN OLD PAINT — ACCOMPANIMENT

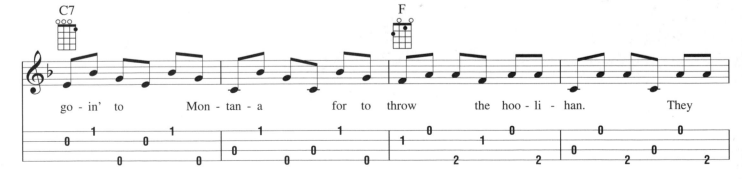

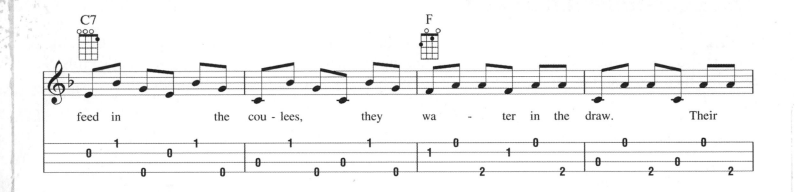

feed in the cou - lees, they wa - ter in the draw. Their

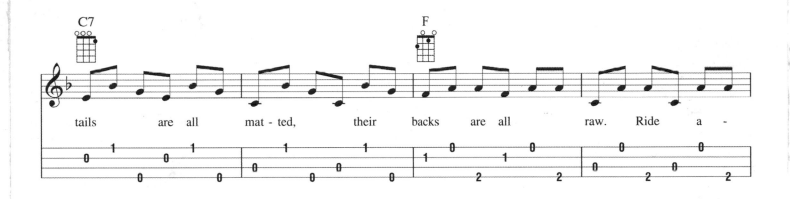

tails are all mat - ted, their backs are all raw. Ride a -

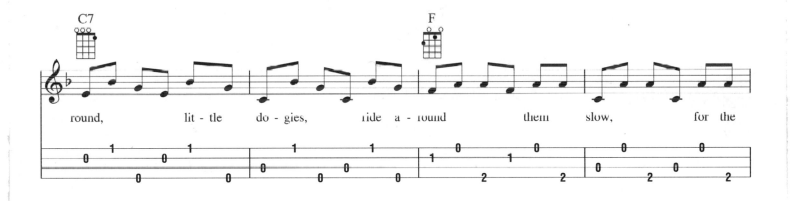

round, lit - tle do - gies, ride a - round them slow, for the

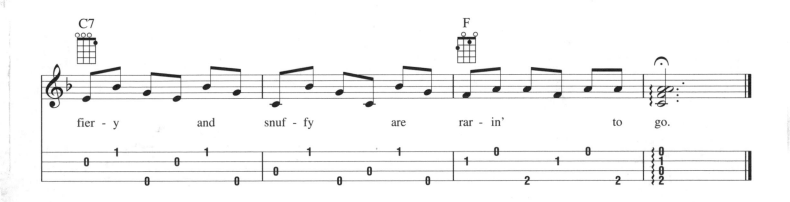

fier - y and snuf - fy are rar - in' to go.

THE CLAWHAMMER STRUM

The Fred Sokolow book, *Ukulele Bluegrass*—also published by Hal Leonard—shows many more three-finger rolls. It also teaches the banjo-style *clawhammer* accompaniment pattern as shown below. Practice this pattern and then use it on the old Carter Family country tune, "Will the Circle Be Unbroken."

- Pick down on the second string with your index finger.
- Brush or *strum* down on the first, second, and third strings with your index finger (indicated by the arrow).
- Pick the fourth string with your thumb.
- Repeat all three strokes changing the first step (second string/index finger) to third string/index finger.

TRACK 13
(0:00)

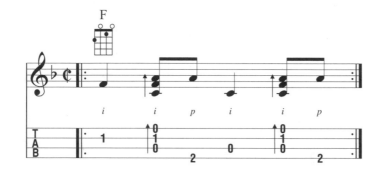

To give the strum variety, the index finger can change notes. It sounds good when you start the pattern by picking the root note (e.g., the F note in an F chord). The rhythm should have a galloping sound (listen to the track for timing). Some people prefer to pick *up* with the index finger, rather than down, to begin this strum. Try it both ways and see which is easier for you.

TRACK 13
(0:07)

WILL THE CIRCLE BE UNBROKEN — CLAWHAMMER ACCOMPANIMENT

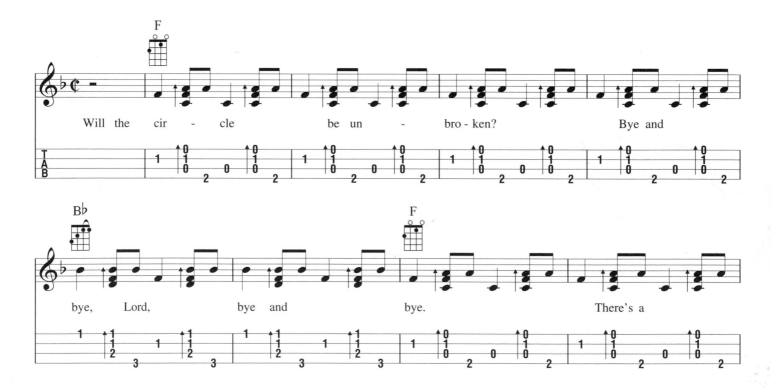

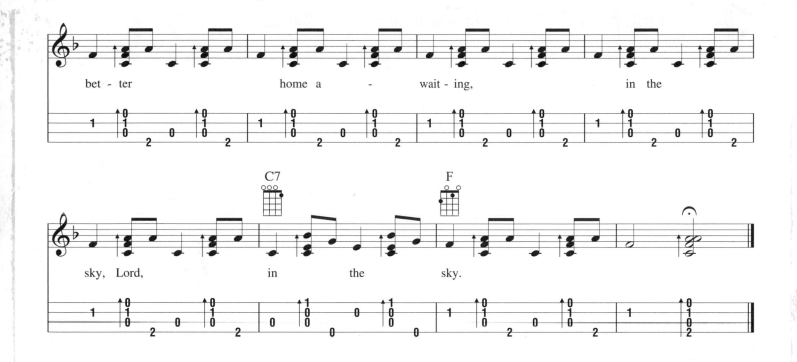

bet - ter   home a - wait-ing,   in the

sky, Lord,   in   the   sky.

THE CLAWHAMMER STRUM IN 3/4 TIME

The clawhammer strum can also be adapted to waltz (3/4) time.

- Pick down on the first string with your index finger.
- Brush down on the first, second, and third strings with your index finger.
- Pick the fourth string with your thumb.
- Brush down on the first, second, and third strings with your index finger.
- Pick the fourth string with your thumb.

TRACK 14
(0:00)

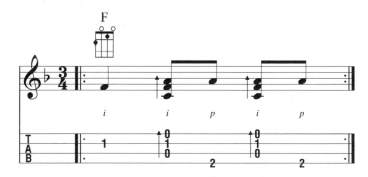

Just like the clawhammer strum in 4/4 time, the index finger can pick any string—preferably the root—and it can alternate strings in any way that sounds good. Try this pattern on "I Ride an Old Paint."

I RIDE AN OLD PAINT — CLAWHAMMER ACCOMPANIMENT

Fingerstyle Lead
(Chord Soloing)

When you play chords and melody at the same time, you're chord soloing. Some call it *chord melody* style. Whatever you call it, it's a very full use of the instrument that works well for country, blues, jazz, or any kind of music. Here are a few general concepts:

- Chord soloists don't play a chord for every single note. They may play a series of single notes—three, four, or five notes—and only one of the notes is harmonized with a chord.

- Usually, the chord melody player tries to make the melody note the highest note in the chord because the highest note tends to stand out.

- The ukulele doesn't sustain long notes like an organ, violin, or wind instrument, so the player fills in the space between long, sustained notes with strums or arpeggios—picking the notes of a chord individually, like a harp.

STRUMS AND PINCHES

Chords can be played by strumming downward with your thumb. They can also be played as a *pinch* in which your finger picks up on the melody note while the thumb brushes down on the lower strings.

BUILDING A CHORD MELODY SOLO

When you're creating a chord melody solo, it may be helpful to do it in three stages:

1. Strum through the song's chords.

2. Find the melody notes.

3. Put the two together.

For example, strum the chords to "Amazing Grace" in the key of F, as shown on the following page.

AMAZING GRACE IN F — CHORDS

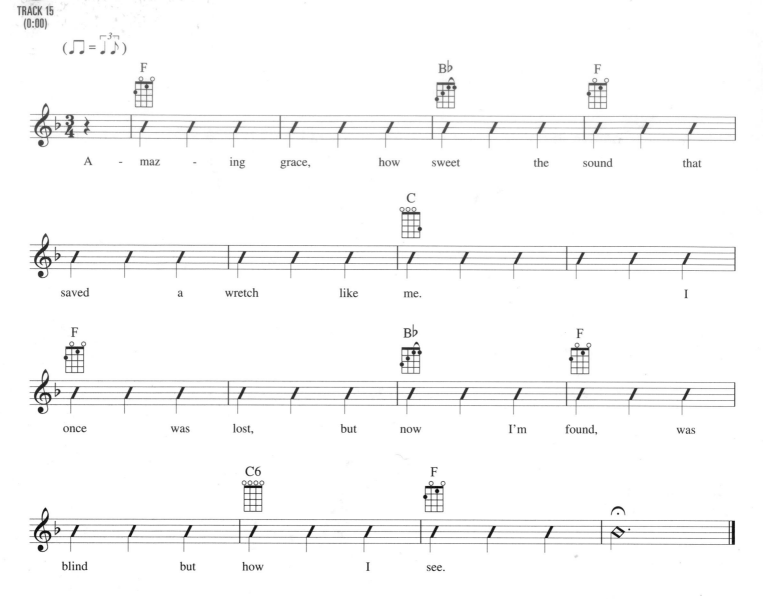

A - maz - ing grace, how sweet the sound that

saved a wretch like me. I

once was lost, but now I'm found, was

blind but how I see.

Now find the melody notes. This is easy to do if you are very familiar with the major scale of your key (F, in this case). All or most of the melody notes will be in that scale. Play the F major scale over and over until you know where all of the notes are. Next, try to find the melody to "Amazing Grace."

F Major Scale

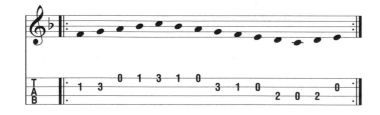

AMAZING GRACE IN F — MELODY

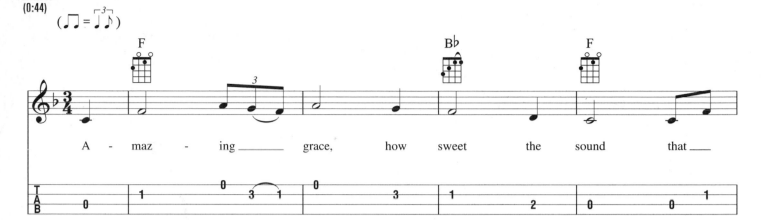

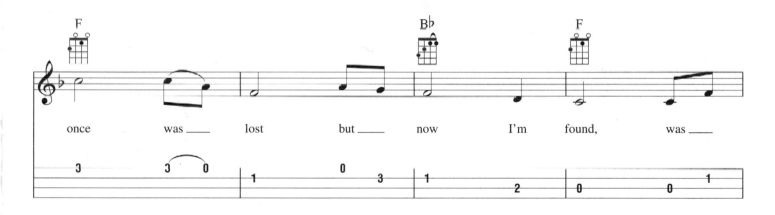

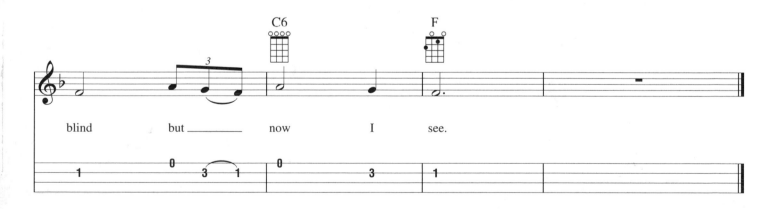

Now, put the melody and chords together.

- In addition to being F major scale notes, most of the melody notes are in the chord being played at that moment.
- *Fill-in strums* are sometimes added to cover the occasional long pauses between melody notes.

AMAZING GRACE IN F — CHORD MELODY SOLO

Here's the same tune in the key of G, starting with the chords.

AMAZING GRACE IN G — CHORDS

TRACK 16
(0:00)

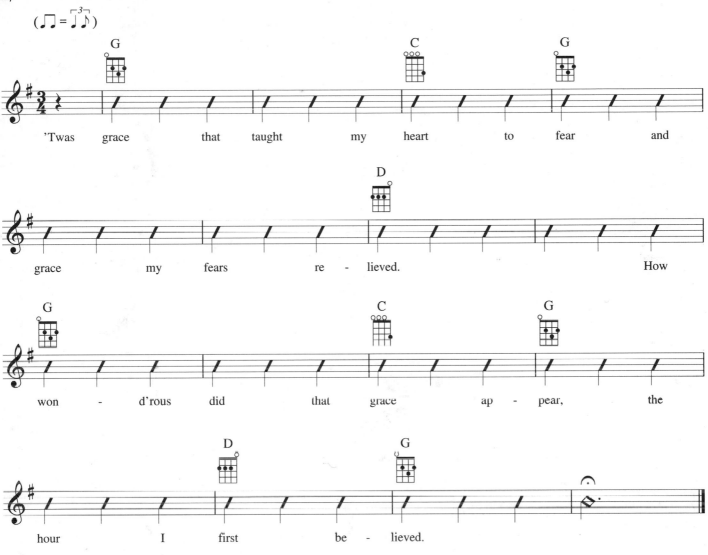

Play the G major scale over and over until you know where all of the notes are. Next, try to find the melody to "Amazing Grace" on your own.

G Major Scale

TRACK 16
(0:32)

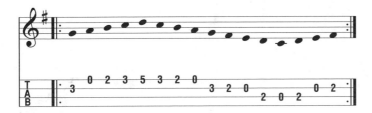

You'll need to use an *up-the-neck chord*—because of a high note on the first string/5th fret—when putting together the melody and chords here.

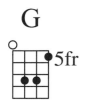

G

5fr

AMAZING GRACE IN G — CHORD MELODY SOLO

UP-THE-NECK CHORDS

First-position chords are the easy chords in the first few frets which include some open strings. *Moveable chords* can be played all over the fretboard because they don't include open strings. For example, the B♭ chord is moveable. It can be played higher up the neck so that it becomes a B chord, a C chord, a C♯ chord, and so on.

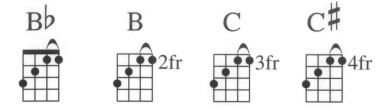

The previous version of "Amazing Grace" (Track 16) includes a moveable chord (G at the 5th fret) because a high melody note has to be supported with a G chord. This raises the question: how do you find these up-the-neck chords? Melodies will often take you beyond the 5th fret and you'll need to locate chords up there! Do you have to memorize every possible chord on the ukulele?

You can become familiar with up-the-neck chords by using them repeatedly, just like everything else on a musical instrument. However, there are some shortcuts to finding your way around the fretboard. Here's one: *memorize all the C and F chords*. Start by playing all C chords.

C Major Chords

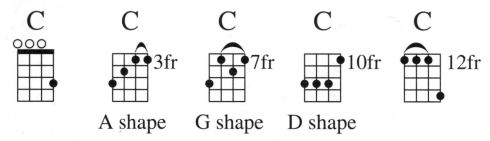

The names of the moveable chord shapes above—A, G, and D—come from their first position uses.

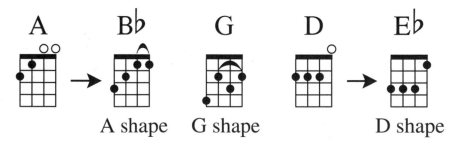

You can use the A, G, and D shapes to play all the F chords.

F Major Chords

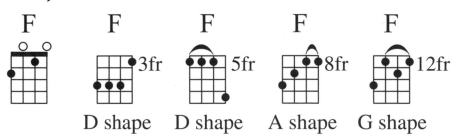

The following exercise will help you memorize all of the C and F major chords.

C AND F CHORD WALTZ

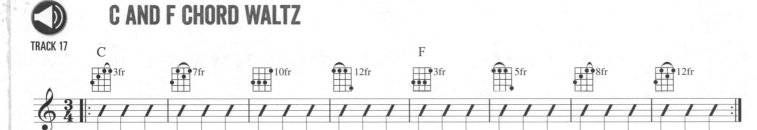

Once you know all of the C chords, you also know the B chords (one fret lower) and the D chords (two frets higher). Likewise, once you know all of the F chords, you know where the E chords are (one fret lower) or the G chords (two frets higher). You can extend this type of thinking to include all of the major chords: Bb is one fret below B, A is two frets above G, and so on.

TURNING MAJORS INTO MINORS

You can extend your moveable chord knowledge even further if you learn how to turn the three moveable major chord shapes into minor shapes.

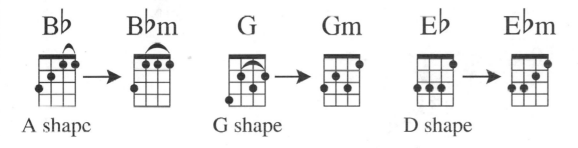

Use this information to chart out all of the Cm and Fm chords.

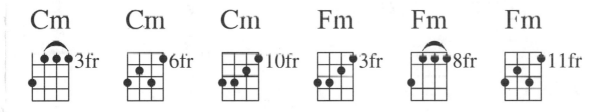

TURNING MAJORS INTO 7THS

If you know how to turn the moveable major chord shapes into 7th chords, you'll know how to play the three types of chords—major, minor, and 7th—all over the fretboard.

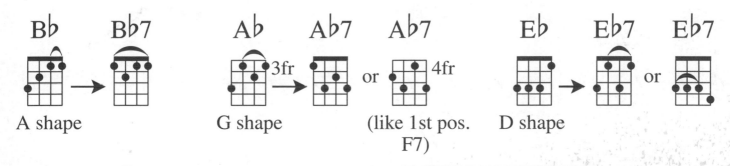

Here are all of the C7 and F7 chords.

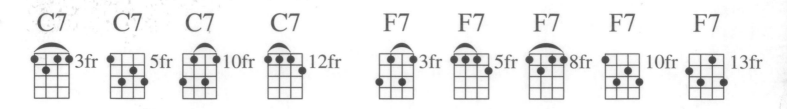

Learning this fretboard information is a process. It takes a lot of repetition and some thought, but it pays off, big time. Most of the chord melody solos in this book, and the chord melody solos you'll invent on your own, will require the use of some up-the-neck chords. You've got to start somewhere, and learning all of the C and F chords is as good a place as any.

SOME SIMPLE CHORD SOLOS

Back in the key of G, here's a simple chord melody solo for the Hawaiian tune, "Aloha 'Oe." This is one every ukulele player should know!

ALOHA 'OE IN G — CHORDS

TRACK 18
(0:00)

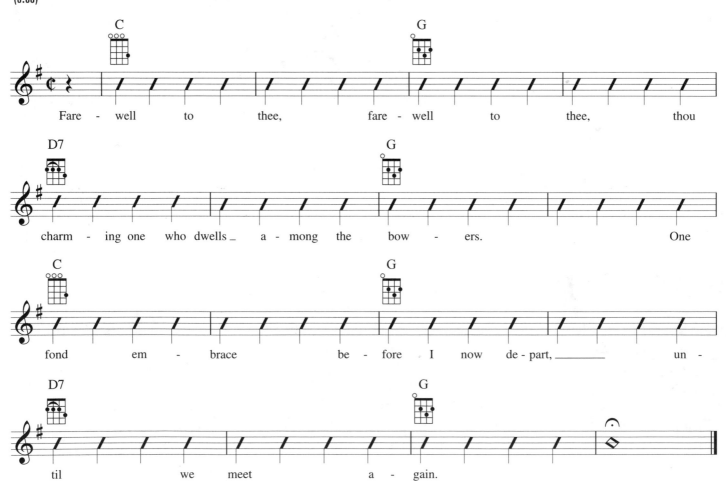

ALOHA 'OE IN G — MELODY

Notice how useful the fourth string is for playing melodies. Its practical use is more apparent when you play melody and chords together, as shown on the next page. In this arrangement, strums are added between melody notes to fill out the rhythm. This system works well for tunes that are in cut time.

ALOHA 'OE IN G — CHORD MELODY SOLO

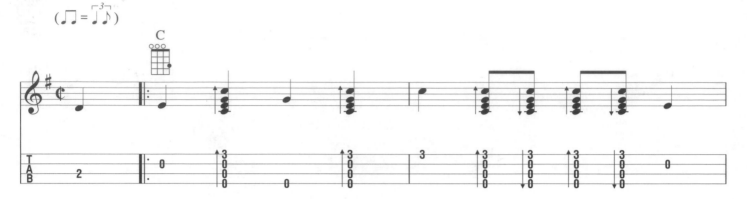

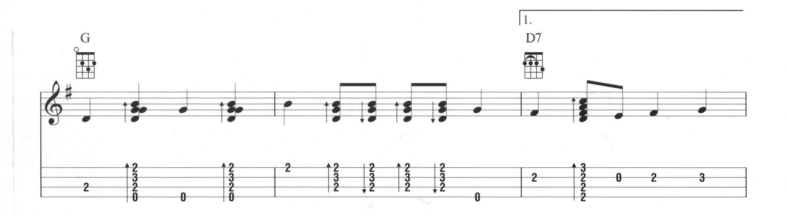

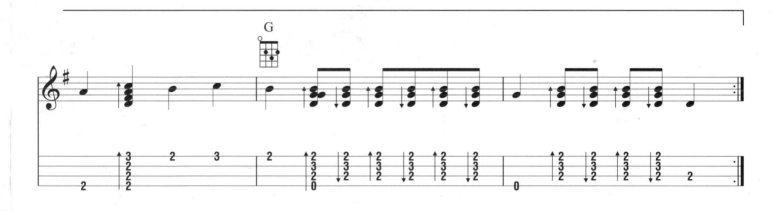

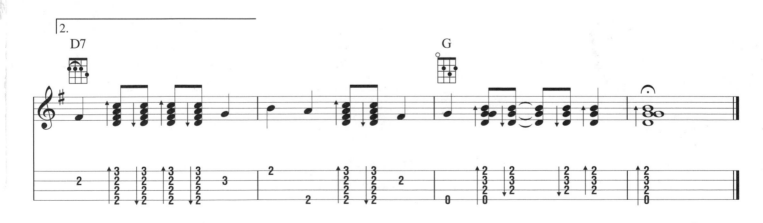

Now for more of a challenge, here's the same song in the key of B♭. First, here is the chord progression in B♭.

ALOHA 'OE IN B♭ — CHORDS

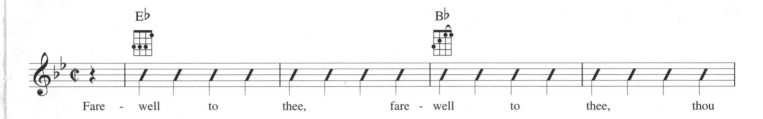

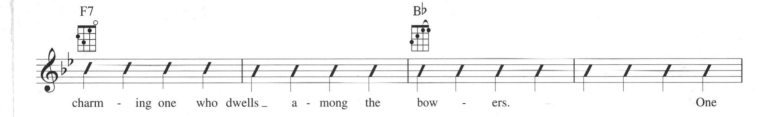

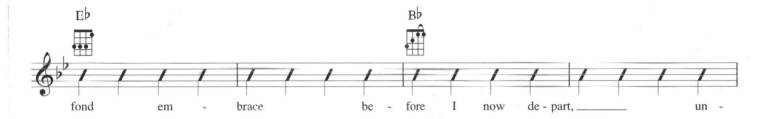

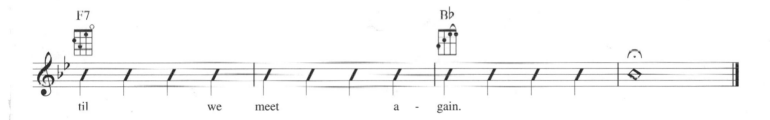

Familiarize yourself with the B♭ major scale notes and then play the melody.

B♭ Major Scale

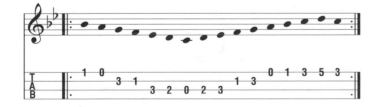

ALOHA 'OE IN B♭ — MELODY

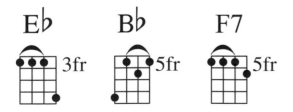

TRACK 19
(0:46)

When you put the melody and chords together, you need the following up-the-neck chords to support those high melody notes:

E♭   B♭   F7

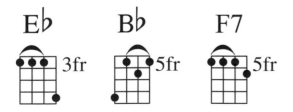

TRACK 19
(1:15)

ALOHA 'OE IN B♭ — CHORD MELODY SOLO

CLAWHAMMER SOLOS

Back to the familiar key of G, here's the chord progression and melody of the old cowboy song, "Red River Valley."

 RED RIVER VALLEY IN G — CHORDS

TRACK 20
(0:00)

Come and sit by my side if you love me. Do not

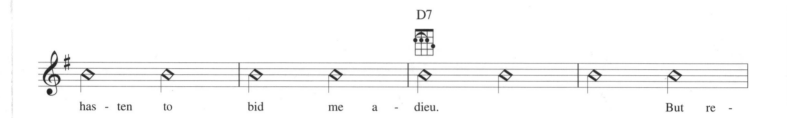

has - ten to bid me a - dieu. But re -

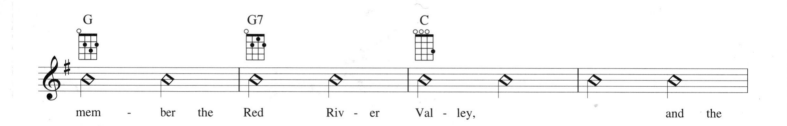

mem - ber the Red Riv - er Val - ley, and the

cow - boy who loved you so true.

RED RIVER VALLEY IN G — MELODY

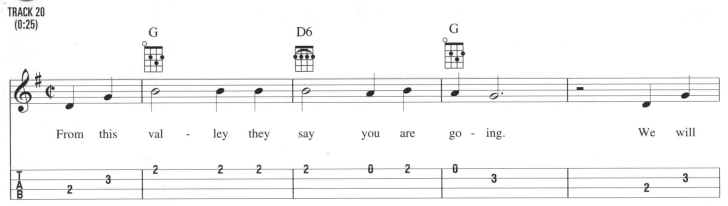

From this val - ley they say you are go - ing. We will

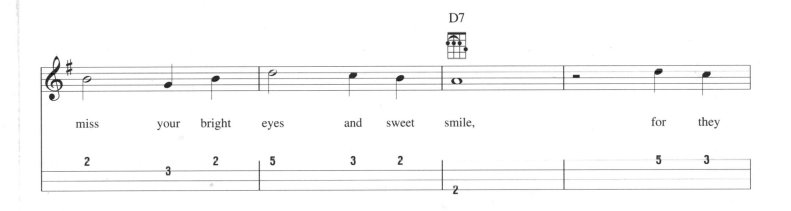

miss your bright eyes and sweet smile, for they

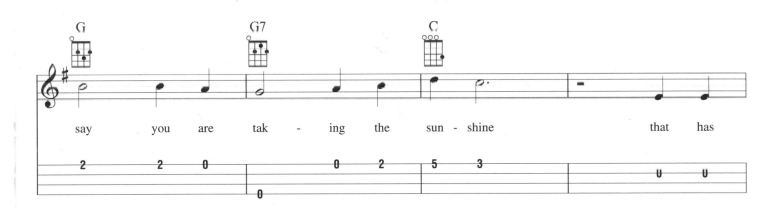

say you are tak - ing the sun - shine that has

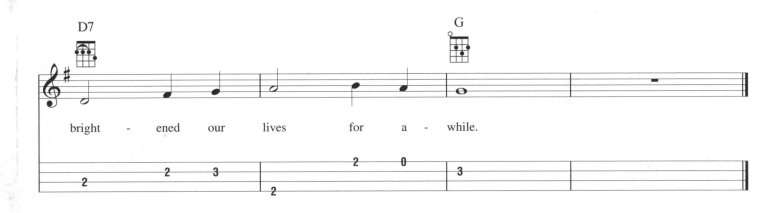

bright - ened our lives for a - while.

Now put them together for a simple chord melody solo.

RED RIVER VALLEY IN G — CHORD MELODY SOLO

TRACK 21
(0:00)

Here's a way to alter the same chord melody solo by adding the clawhammer strum that you learned in the accompaniment chapter (Track 13).

RED RIVER VALLEY IN G — CLAWHAMMER SOLO

TRACK 21
(0:25)

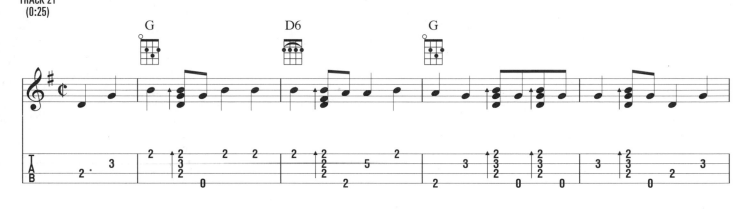

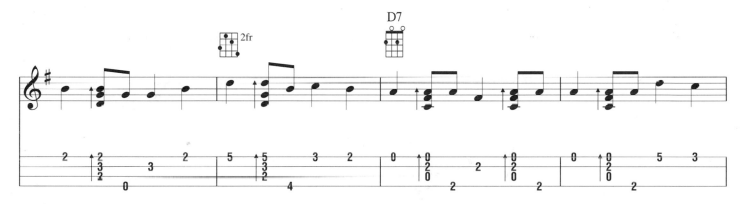

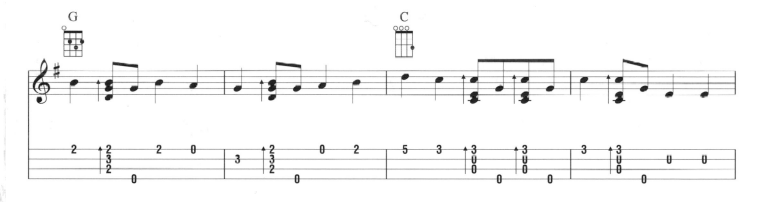

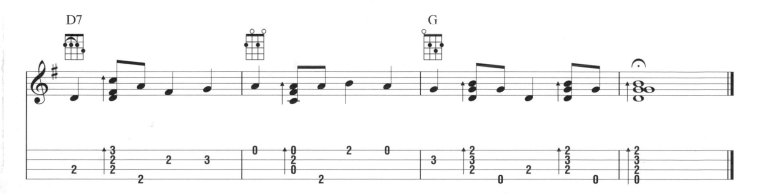

Another Hawaiian standard, "On the Beach at Waikiki," lends itself to the clawhammer style. Here's the chord progression followed by a chord melody solo in G.

ON THE BEACH AT WAIKIKI IN G — CHORDS

TRACK 22
(0:00)

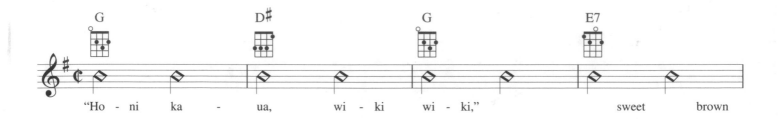

"Ho - ni ka - ua, wi - ki wi - ki," sweet brown

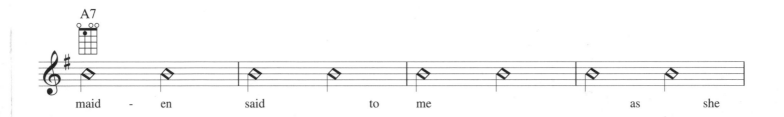

maid - en said to me as she

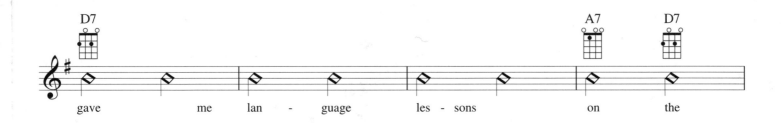

gave me lan - guage les - sons on the

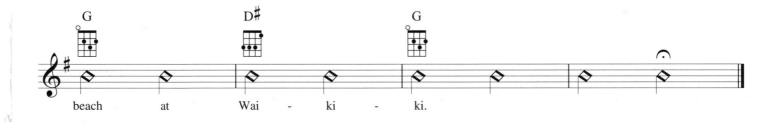

beach at Wai - ki - ki.

ON THE BEACH AT WAIKIKI IN G — CHORD MELODY SOLO

Now mix in some clawhammer strumming.

TRACK 22
(0:40)

ON THE BEACH AT WAIKIKI IN G — CLAWHAMMER SOLO

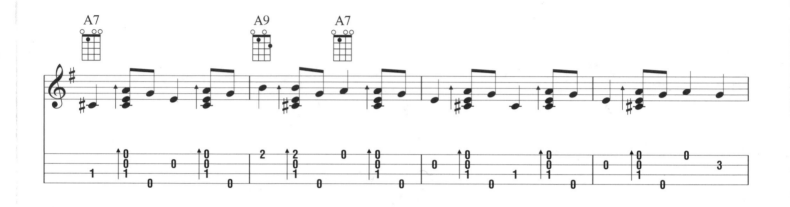

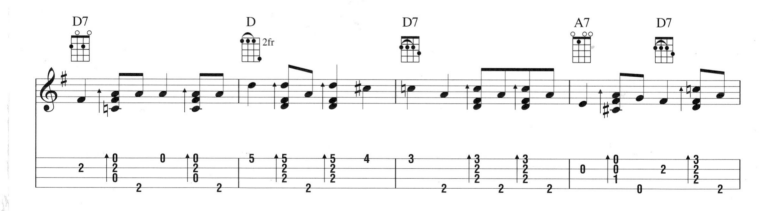

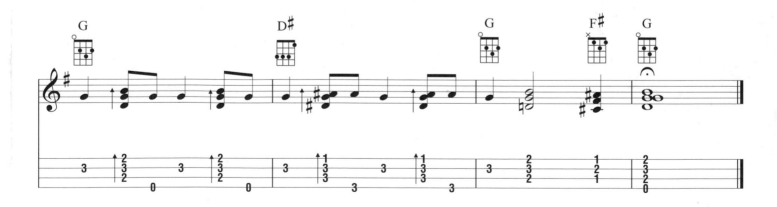

Since most of the chord shapes in this arrangement are moveable, it doesn't take too much adjustment to move this solo up a fret and play it in A♭.

TRACK 22
(1:02)

ON THE BEACH AT WAIKIKI IN A♭ — CLAWHAMMER SOLO

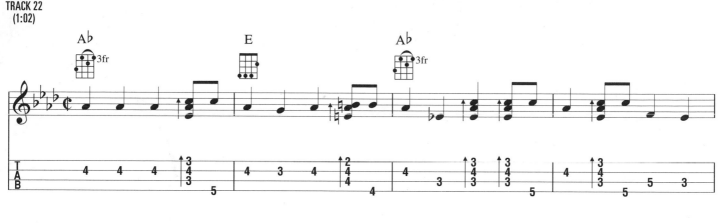

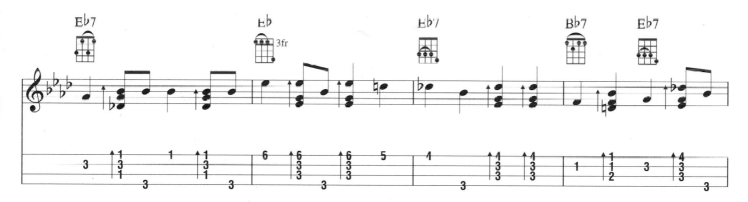

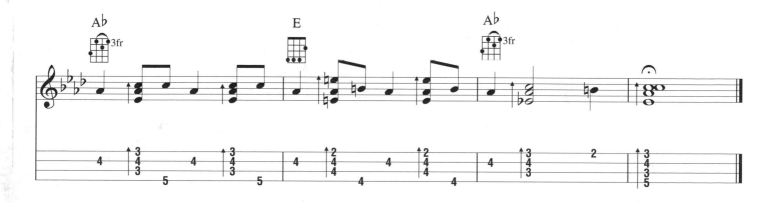

A CLAWHAMMER SOLO IN WALTZ TIME

The folk song, "I Never Will Marry," is well suited to the 3/4 time clawhammer strum (Track 14).

I NEVER WILL MARRY IN D — CHORDS

TRACK 23
(0:00)

Practice the D major scale, then play "I Never Will Marry" as a simple chord melody solo.

D Major Scale

TRACK 23
(0:37)

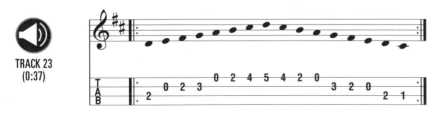

I NEVER WILL MARRY IN D — CHORD MELODY SOLO

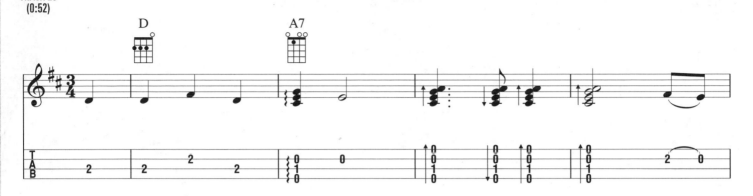

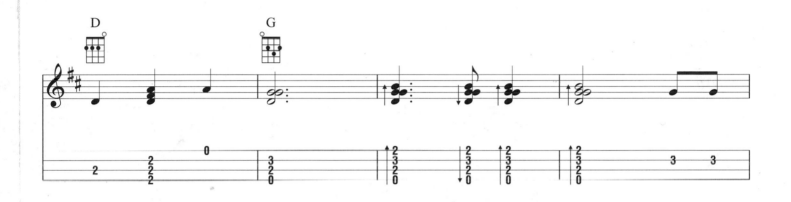

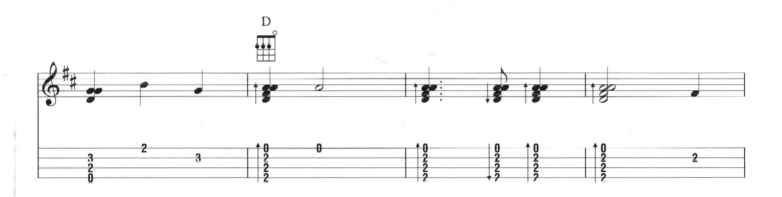

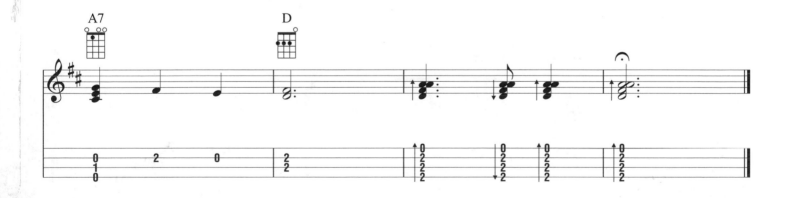

Now add some clawhammer strums.

I NEVER WILL MARRY IN D — CLAWHAMMER SOLO

TRACK 23
(1:13)

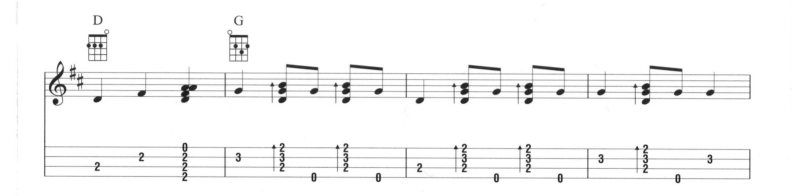

A 6/8 TIME SOLO

"Rising Sun Blues" has been recorded and performed by folk, blues, country, and rock artists. The 6/8 time version that follows has many sustained melody notes, so a good deal of fill-in strumming is required. Here are the basic chords and a chord melody solo.

Note: The Dm scale has the same notes as the F major scale.

TRACK 24
(0:00)

RISING SUN BLUES IN Dm — CHORDS

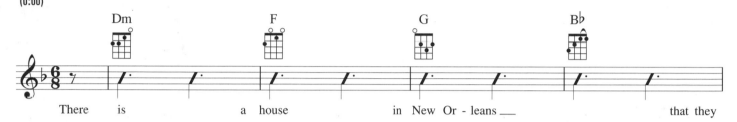

There is a house in New Or - leans ___ that they

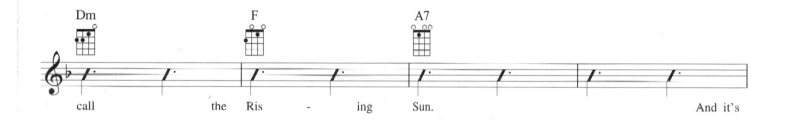

call the Ris - ing Sun. And it's

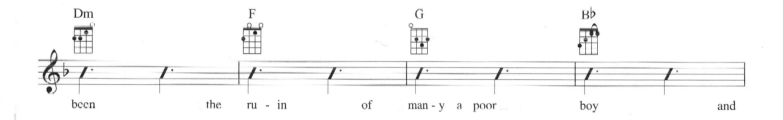

been the ru - in of man - y a poor boy and

God I know I'm one.

Now add the fill-in strumming.

TRACK 24
(1:01)

RISING SUN BLUES IN Dm — CHORD MELODY SOLO WITH FILLS

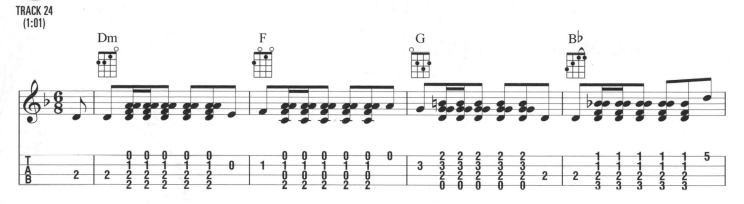

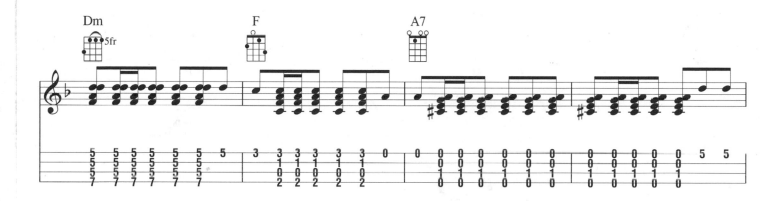

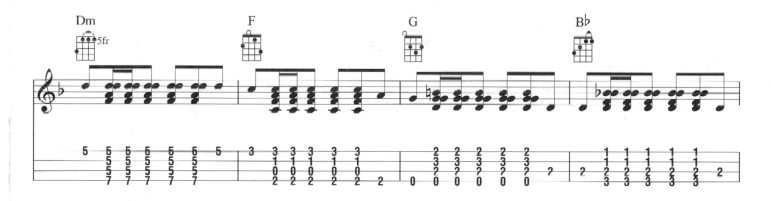

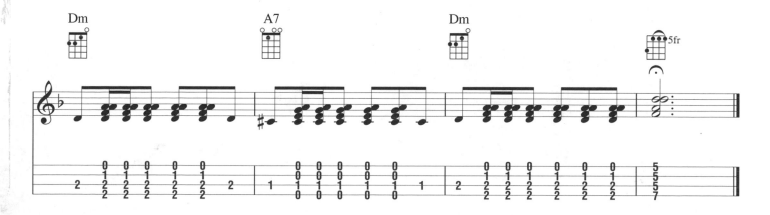

MORE CHORD SOLOS

The Tin Pan Alley standard, "Shine On, Harvest Moon," is fairly easy to arrange on the ukulele. Here's the chord progression and chord melody solo in the key of G.

SHINE ON, HARVEST MOON IN G — CHORDS

TRACK 25
(0:00)

SHINE ON, HARVEST MOON IN G — CHORD MELODY SOLO

If you move everything up a couple of frets—to the key of A—a few more moveable chords are needed.

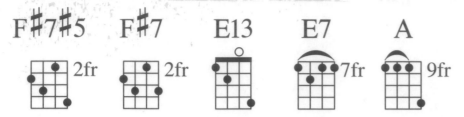

However, much of the arrangement remains the same.

SHINE ON, HARVEST MOON IN A — CHORD MELODY SOLO

TRACK 25
(1:11)

MONOTONE THUMB ACCOMPANIMENT

W. C. Handy's "St. Louis Blues," written in 1914, has become one of the most famous blues and jazz standards of all time. It continues to be performed and recorded by artists of all genres. The first part of the song is a standard 12-bar blues with a few chord variations thrown in.

The chord melody solo arrangement below uses a *monotone thumb* accompaniment. The melody is played on the first and second strings by the index finger—which picks up on the strings—while the thumb brushes down on the lower strings for accompaniment on every beat. This works well with many blues tunes.

First, get acquainted with the chords and the melody of the tune.

ST. LOUIS BLUES IN A — CHORDS

TRACK 26
(0:00)

Practice the A major scale then play the melody. Notice that, like many blues songs, this tune includes several *blue notes* that are not part of the major scale; especially *flatted sevenths* and *flatted thirds*.

A Major Scale

TRACK 26
(0:29)

Blue Notes in the Key of A

 ST. LOUIS BLUES IN A — MELODY

TRACK 26
(0:41)

I hate to see ___ that eve-ning sun go down. ___

Hate to see ___ that eve-ning sun go down, __

'cause my ba - by

has done left this town. ___

ST. LOUIS BLUES IN A — CHORD MELODY SOLO

THE FOURTH STRING AS FILLER

Sometimes you can create a bouncy rhythm by playing the melody with your fingers on the high strings while picking the fourth string with your thumb—between the melody notes. The 1917 vaudeville song, "Darktown Strutter's Ball," has a rhythm that suits this technique. The song is an old jazz standard. On the next page is a basic chord melody solo in the key of C. As usual, practice the C major scale and strum the chords to the song before playing the chord melody.

C Major Scale

TRACK 27
(0:00)

DARKTOWN STRUTTER'S BALL IN C — CHORDS

TRACK 27
(0:11)

DARKTOWN STRUTTER'S BALL IN C — MELODY

Now, add those thumb/fourth string filler notes.

DARKTOWN STRUTTER'S BALL IN C — CHORD MELODY SOLO

TRACK 27
(1:32)

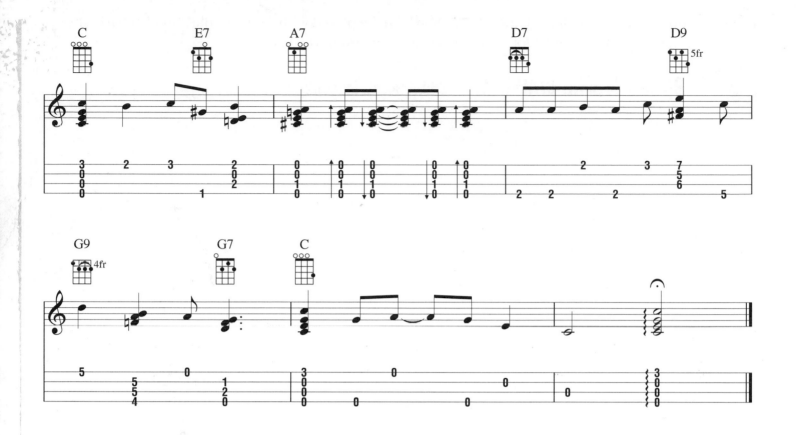

THREE-FINGER ROLLS AS FILLER

You learned some three-finger rolls in the "Fingerstyle Accompaniment" chapter. These same rolls can be played as filler between melody notes in a chord melody solo. They are especially useful in songs with cut-time rhythm.

The roll introduced in Track 10 is called a *forward roll* by banjo players. Any pattern that moves in this direction over and over—like the examples below—is a forward roll.

TRACK 28
(0:00)

The 19th century murder ballad, "Banks of the Ohio," can be played with forward rolls. Here's a basic chords-and-melody version of the country/old-time/bluegrass standard in the key of G.

BANKS OF THE OHIO IN G — CHORDS AND MELODY

TRACK 28
(0:33)

Now add the forward rolls.

BANKS OF THE OHIO IN G — SOLO WITH FORWARD ROLLS

TRACK 28
(0:55)

The 1920 pop song, "Whispering," has been recorded by over 700 artists, including rock and disco versions. Here's a basic chord melody solo arrangement in the key of C followed by a version that is enhanced by forward rolls, as well as some thumb/fourth string filler notes.

WHISPERING IN C — CHORD MELODY SOLO

TRACK 29
(0:00)

WHISPERING IN C — SOLO WITH FORWARD ROLLS

MORE CHORDS! (JAZZ)

Many Tin Pan Alley songs from the early 1900s—like the later jazz tunes of the 1920s through the early 1950s—include altered chords such as: 6ths, 9ths, 13ths, diminished, and augmented chords. The next two tunes—both nearly a hundred years old—feature many of these jazz chords. And both tunes suit the ukulele chord melody style beautifully!

"Poor Butterfly" was inspired by the Puccini opera *Madame Butterfly*. It was very popular in 1917, a year after it was written. The song experienced a revival in the 1950s when the vocal group the Hilltoppers' charted in the Top 20 with their version. This arrangement in B♭ includes many moveable chords.

Here are the new, jazzy chords you will encounter in this arrangement. Many of them are slightly altered versions of minor, major, or seventh chords you have already played. For example, B♭ add9 is just B♭ with one note added by the little finger:

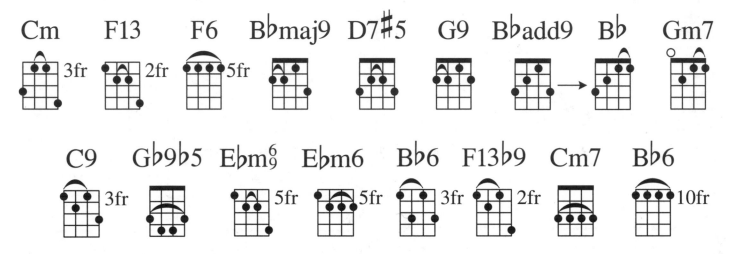

 ## POOR BUTTERFLY IN B♭ — CHORD MELODY SOLO

TRACK 30

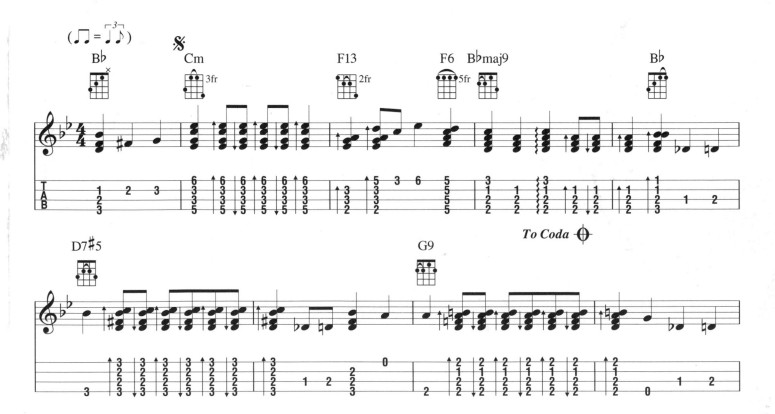

70 **FINGERSTYLE UKULELE**

"For Me and My Gal" was also written in 1917 and was already an old standard when the Judy Garland/Gene Kelly movie by the same name was released in 1942. The following chord melody solo arrangement in G contains plenty of jazz chords, but most of them are the same shapes you've used before in "Poor Butterfly." Here are a few new chord shapes.

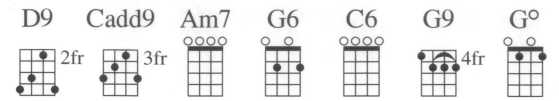

FOR ME AND MY GAL IN G — CHORD MELODY SOLO

TRACK 31

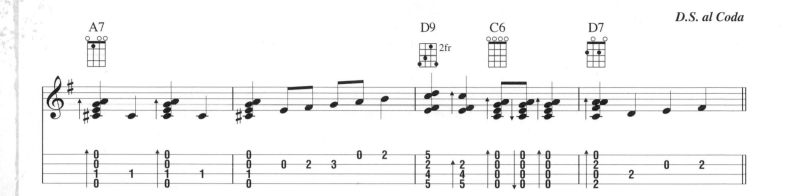

Where to Go from Here

After learning the fingerpicking patterns, techniques, and chord melody solos in this book, try making up your own fingerstyle solos. Just start with simple, three-chord tunes. Also, try accompanying some of your favorite songs with fingerpicking patterns in addition to strumming.

To grow further as a fingerstyle uke player:

LISTEN TO GREAT FINGERSTYLE UKULELE PLAYERS

Eddie Kamae, Lyle Ritz, Herb Ohta, James Hill, John King, Bill Tapia, and Jake Shimabukuro are all ukulele fingerstyle virtuosos of renown who have recorded and performed in recent years, so their work is readily available.

Roy Smeck, Cliff Edwards (Ukulele Ike), and Ernest Ka'ai are great fingerstyle ukulele players of yesteryear and pioneers in the field. They are well represented on YouTube and many of their recordings are still available.

READ MORE UKULELE INSTRUCTION BOOKS

Fred Sokolow's book/CD, *Fretboard Roadmaps for Ukulele*, published by Hal Leonard, helps you locate chords all over the fretboard, understand chord progressions and how to play them, and is filled with info that enhances your understanding of how the ukulele works overall.

Here are some more relevant Sokolow/Hal Leonard books/CDs:

101 Tips for Ukulele includes musical shortcuts, practicing tips, historical info, and all kinds of fun and helpful facts to expand your ukulele consciousness.

Blues Ukulele features chord melody arrangements of 16 great blues standards, as well as strum-along lead (single line) sheets.

Bluegrass Ukulele has three-finger picking arrangements, clawhammer arrangements, and strum-along lead sheets for 21 bluegrass standards.

A FINAL WORD

Anything is possible on the ukulele. Today's virtuosos are playing every type of music you can imagine, from classical to R&B, Latin music to bluegrass, pop, and jazz. Stretch out and try something new!

Good luck and happy picking and strumming!

Chord Dictionary

Here are all the chords used in this book:

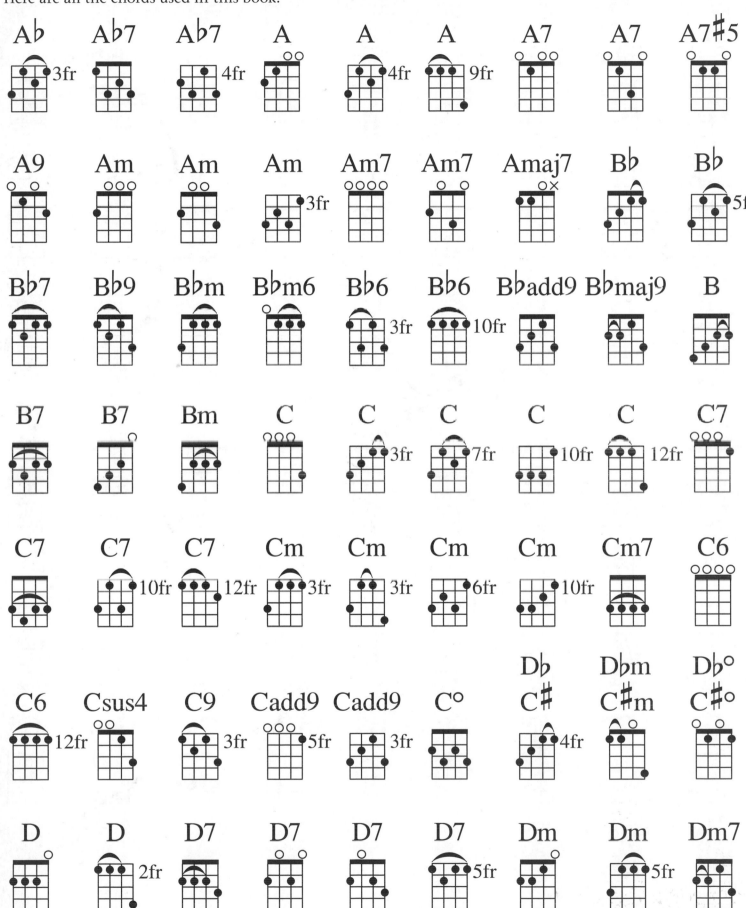

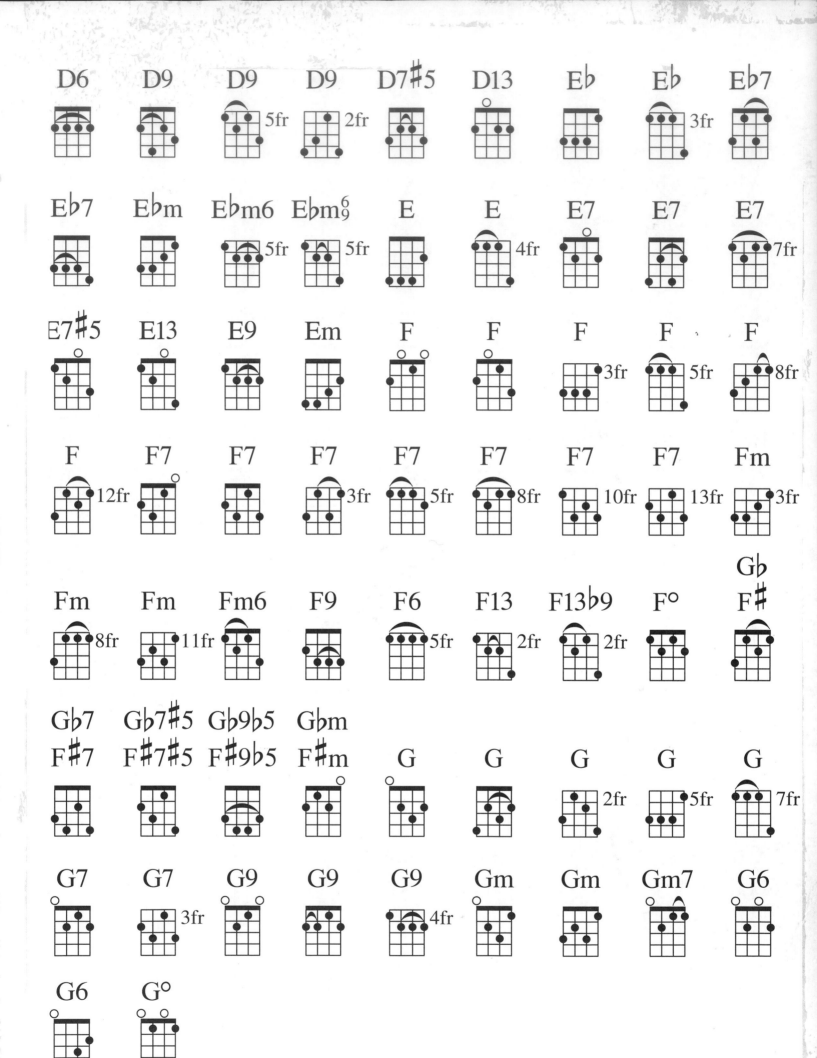

About the Author

Fred Sokolow is best known as the author of over 150 instructional and transcription books and DVDs for guitar, banjo, Dobro, mandolin, lap steel, and ukulele. Fred has long been a well-known West Coast, multi-string performer and recording artist, particularly on the acoustic music scene. The diverse musical genres covered in his books and DVDs, along with several bluegrass, jazz, and rock CDs he has released, demonstrate his mastery of many musical styles. Whether he's playing Delta bottleneck blues, bluegrass or old-time banjo, '30s swing guitar, Hawaiian ukulele, or screaming rock solos, he does it with authenticity and passion.

Fred's other ukulele books include:

- *Fretboard Roadmaps for Ukulele*, book/CD (with Jim Beloff), Hal Leonard Corporation
- *Blues Ukulele*, book/CD, Flea Market Music, distributed by Hal Leonard Corporation
- *Bluegrass Ukulele*, book/CD, Flea Market Music, distributed by Hal Leonard Corporation
- *101 Ukulele Tips*, book/CD, Hal Leonard Corporation

Email Fred with any questions about this or his other ukulele books at: Sokolowmusic.com.

HAL•LEONARD® UKULELE PLAY-ALONG

Now you can play your favorite songs on your uke with great-sounding backing tracks to help you sound like a bona fide pro! The audio also features playback tools so you can adjust the tempo without changing the pitch and loop challenging parts.

1. POP HITS
00701451 Book/CD Pack $15.99

3. HAWAIIAN FAVORITES
00701453 Book/Online Audio $14.99

4. CHILDREN'S SONGS
00701454 Book/Online Audio $14.99

5. CHRISTMAS SONGS
00701696 Book/CD Pack $12.99

6. LENNON & MCCARTNEY
00701723 Book/Online Audio $12.99

7. DISNEY FAVORITES
00701724 Book/Online Audio $14.99

8. CHART HITS
00701745 Book/CD Pack $15.99

9. THE SOUND OF MUSIC
00701784 Book/CD Pack $14.99

10. MOTOWN
00701964 Book/CD Pack $12.99

11. CHRISTMAS STRUMMING
00702458 Book/Online Audio $12.99

12. BLUEGRASS FAVORITES
00702584 Book/CD Pack $12.99

13. UKULELE SONGS
00702599 Book/CD Pack $12.99

14. JOHNNY CASH
00702615 Book/Online Audio $15.99

15. COUNTRY CLASSICS
00702834 Book/CD Pack $12.99

16. STANDARDS
00702835 Book/CD Pack $12.99

17. POP STANDARDS
00702836 Book/CD Pack $12.99

18. IRISH SONGS
00703086 Book/Online Audio $12.99

19. BLUES STANDARDS
00703087 Book/CD Pack $12.99

20. FOLK POP ROCK
00703088 Book/CD Pack $12.99

21. HAWAIIAN CLASSICS
00703097 Book/CD Pack $12.99

22. ISLAND SONGS
00703098 Book/CD Pack $12.99

23. TAYLOR SWIFT
00221966 Book/Online Audio $16.99

24. WINTER WONDERLAND
00101871 Book/CD Pack $12.99

25. GREEN DAY
00110398 Book/CD Pack $14.99

26. BOB MARLEY
00110399 Book/Online Audio $14.99

27. TIN PAN ALLEY
00116358 Book/CD Pack $12.99

28. STEVIE WONDER
00116736 Book/CD Pack $14.99

29. OVER THE RAINBOW & OTHER FAVORITES
00117076 Book/Online Audio $15.99

30. ACOUSTIC SONGS
00122336 Book/CD Pack $14.99

31. JASON MRAZ
00124166 Book/CD Pack $14.99

32. TOP DOWNLOADS
00127507 Book/CD Pack $14.99

33. CLASSICAL THEMES
00127892 Book/Online Audio $14.99

34. CHRISTMAS HITS
00128602 Book/CD Pack $14.99

35. SONGS FOR BEGINNERS
00129009 Book/Online Audio $14.99

36. ELVIS PRESLEY HAWAII
00138199 Book/Online Audio $14.99

37. LATIN
00141191 Book/Online Audio $14.99

38. JAZZ
00141192 Book/Online Audio $14.99

39. GYPSY JAZZ
00146559 Book/Online Audio $15.99

40. TODAY'S HITS
00160845 Book/Online Audio $14.99

HAL•LEONARD®
www.halleonard.com

Prices, contents, and availability subject to change without notice.

1021
483

The Best Collections for Ukulele

The Best Songs Ever

70 songs have now been arranged for ukulele. Includes: Always • Bohemian Rhapsody • Memory • My Favorite Things • Over the Rainbow • Piano Man • What a Wonderful World • Yesterday • You Raise Me Up • and more.

00282413 . . . . $17.99

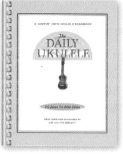

Campfire Songs for Ukulele

30 favorites to sing as you roast marshmallows and strum your uke around the campfire. Includes: God Bless the U.S.A. • Hallelujah • The House of the Rising Sun • I Walk the Line • Puff the Magic Dragon • Wagon Wheel • You Are My Sunshine • and more.

00129170 . . . . $14.99

The Daily Ukulele

arr. Liz and Jim Beloff

Strum a different song everyday with easy arrangements of 365 of your favorite songs in one big songbook! Includes favorites by the Beatles, Beach Boys, and Bob Dylan, folk songs, pop songs, kids' songs, Christmas carols, and Broadway and Hollywood tunes, all with a spiral binding for ease of use.

00240356 Original Edition $39.99
00240681 Leap Year Edition $39.99
00119270 Portable Edition $37.50

Disney Hits for Ukulele

Play 23 of your favorite Disney songs on your ukulele. Includes: The Bare Necessities • Cruella De Vil • Do You Want to Build a Snowman? • Kiss the Girl • Lava • Let It Go • Once upon a Dream • A Whole New World • and more.

00151250 . . . . $16.99

Also available:

00291547 **Disney Fun Songs for Ukulele** . . . $16.99
00701708 **Disney Songs for Ukulele** $14.99
00334696 **First 50 Disney Songs on Ukulele** . $16.99

First 50 Songs You Should Play on Ukulele

An amazing collec-tion of 50 accessible, must-know favorites: Edelweiss • Hey, Soul Sister • I Walk the Line • I'm Yours • Imagine • Over the Rainbow • Peaceful Easy Feeling • The Rainbow Connection • Riptide • more.

00149250 . . . . $16.99

Also available:

00292082 **First 50 Melodies on Ukulele** . . . $15.99
00289029 **First 50 Songs on Solo Ukulele** . . $15.99
00347437 **First 50 Songs to Strum on Uke** . $16.99

40 Most Streamed Songs for Ukulele

40 top hits that sound great on uke! Includes: Despacito • Feel It Still • Girls like You • Happier • Havana • High Hopes • The Middle • Perfect • 7 Rings • Shallow • Shape of You • Something Just like This • Stay • Sucker • Sunflower • Sweet but Psycho • Thank U, Next • There's Nothing Holdin' Me Back • Without Me • and more!

00298113 . . . . $17.99

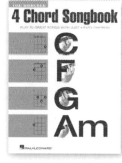

The 4 Chord Songbook

With just 4 chords, you can play 50 hot songs on your ukulele! Songs include: Brown Eyed Girl • Do Wah Diddy Diddy • Hey Ya! • Ho Hey • Jessie's Girl • Let It Be • One Love • Stand by Me • Toes • With or Without You • and many more.

00142050 . . . . $16.99

Also available:

00141143 **The 3-Chord Songbook** $16.99

Pop Songs for Kids

30 easy pop favorites for kids to play on uke, including: Brave • Can't Stop the Feeling! • Feel It Still • Fight Song • Happy • Havana • House of Gold • How Far I'll Go • Let It Go • Remember Me (Ernesto de la Cruz) • Rewrite the Stars • Roar • Shake It Off • Story of My Life • What Makes You Beautiful • and more.

00284415 . . . . $16.99

Simple Songs for Ukulele

50 favorites for standard G-C-E-A ukulele tuning, including: All Along the Watchtower • Can't Help Falling in Love • Don't Worry, Be Happy • Ho Hey • I'm Yours • King of the Road • Sweet Home Alabama • You Are My Sunshine • and more.

00156815 . . . . $14.99

Also available:

00276644 **More Simple Songs for Ukulele** . $14.99

Top Hits of 2020

18 uke-friendly tunes of 2020 are featured in this collection of melody, lyric and chord arrangements in standard G-C-E-A tuning. Includes: Adore You (Harry Styles) • Before You Go (Lewis Capaldi) • Cardigan (Taylor Swift) • Daisies (Katy Perry) • I Dare You (Kelly Clarkson) • Level of Concern (twenty one pilots) • No Time to Die (Billie Eilish) • Rain on Me (Lady Gaga feat. Ariana Grande) • Say So (Doja Cat) • and more.

00355553 . . . . $14.99

Also available:

00302274 **Top Hits of 2019** $14.99

Ukulele: The Most Requested Songs

Strum & Sing Series
Cherry Lane Music

Nearly 50 favorites all expertly arranged for ukulele! Includes: Bubbly • Build Me Up, Buttercup • Cecilia • Georgia on My Mind • Kokomo • L-O-V-E • Your Body Is a Wonderland • and more.

02501453 . . . . $14.99

The Ultimate Ukulele Fake Book

Uke enthusiasts will love this giant, spiral-bound collection of over 400 songs for uke! Includes: Crazy • Dancing Queen • Downtown • Fields of Gold • Happy • Hey Jude • 7 Years • Summertime • Thinking Out Loud • Thriller • Wagon Wheel • and more.

00175500 9" x 12" Edition $45.00
00319997 5.5" x 8.5" Edition $39.99

UKULELE CHORD SONGBOOKS

This series features convenient 6" x 9" books with complete lyrics and chord symbols for dozens of great songs. Each song also includes chord grids at the top of every page and the first notes of the melody for easy reference.

ACOUSTIC ROCK

60 tunes: American Pie • Band on the Run • Catch the Wind • Daydream • Every Rose Has Its Thorn • Hallelujah • Iris • More Than Words • Patience • The Sound of Silence • Space Oddity • Sweet Talkin' Woman • Wake up Little Susie • Who'll Stop the Rain • and more.
00702482 . . . .$15.99

THE BEATLES

100 favorites: Across the Universe • Carry That Weight • Dear Prudence • Good Day Sunshine • Here Comes the Sun • If I Fell • Love Me Do • Michelle • Ob-La-Di, Ob-La-Da • Revolution • Something • Ticket to Ride • We Can Work It Out • and many more.
00703065. . . . .$19.99

BEST SONGS EVER

70 songs: All I Ask of You • Bewitched • Edelweiss • Just the Way You Are • Let It Be • Memory • Moon River • Over the Rainbow • Someone to Watch over Me • Unchained Melody • You Are the Sunshine of My Life • You Raise Me Up • and more.
00117050 . . . .$16.99

CHILDREN'S SONGS

80 classics: Alphabet Song • "C" Is for Cookie • Do-Re-Mi • I'm Popeye the Sailor Man • Mickey Mouse March • Oh! Susanna • Polly Wolly Doodle • Puff the Magic Dragon • The Rainbow Connection • Sing • Three Little Fishies (Itty Bitty Poo) • and many more.
00702473 . . . .$14.99

CHRISTMAS CAROLS

75 favorites: Away in a Manger • Coventry Carol • The First Noel • Good King Wenceslas • Hark! the Herald Angels Sing • I Saw Three Ships • Joy to the World • O Little Town of Bethlehem • Still, Still, Still • Up on the Housetop • What Child Is This? • and more.
00702474 . . . .$14.99

CHRISTMAS SONGS

55 Christmas classics: Do They Know It's Christmas? • Frosty the Snow Man • Happy Xmas (War Is Over) • Jingle-Bell Rock • Little Saint Nick • The Most Wonderful Time of the Year • White Christmas • and more.
00101776 . . . .$14.99

ISLAND SONGS

60 beach party tunes: Blue Hawaii • Day-O (The Banana Boat Song) • Don't Worry, Be Happy • Island Girl • Kokomo • Lovely Hula Girl • Mele Kalikimaka • Red, Red Wine • Surfer Girl • Tiny Bubbles • Ukulele Lady • and many more.
00702471 . . . .$16.99

150 OF THE MOST BEAUTIFUL SONGS EVER

150 melodies: Always • Bewitched • Candle in the Wind • Endless Love • In the Still of the Night • Just the Way You Are • Memory • The Nearness of You • People • The Rainbow Connection • Smile • Unchained Melody • What a Wonderful World • Yesterday • and more.
00117051 . . . .$24.99

PETER, PAUL & MARY

Over 40 songs: And When I Die • Blowin' in the Wind • Goodnight, Irene • If I Had a Hammer (The Hammer Song) • Leaving on a Jet Plane • Puff the Magic Dragon • This Land Is Your Land • We Shall Overcome • Where Have All the Flowers Gone? • and more.
00121822 . . . .$14.99

THREE CHORD SONGS

60 songs: Bad Case of Loving You • Bang a Gong (Get It On) • Blue Suede Shoes • Cecilia • Get Back • Hound Dog • Kiss • Me and Bobby McGee • Not Fade Away • Rock This Town • Sweet Home Chicago • Twist and Shout • You Are My Sunshine • and more.
00702483 . . . .$15.99

TOP HITS

31 hits: The A Team • Born This Way • Forget You • Ho Hey • Jar of Hearts • Little Talks • Need You Now • Rolling in the Deep • Teenage Dream • Titanium • We Are Never Ever Getting Back Together • and more.
00115929 . . . .$14.99

Prices, contents, and availability subject to change without notice.